W9-ASD-232

In the world in which we live it is impossible to hide mistakes from our children. Let's acknowledge those mistakes and work together for the future of our planet.

FRIENDS OF THE EARTH

© 1991 Kim Fernandes (Text and Art)
Design Kim Fernandes
Photography Pat Lacroix

Annick Press Ltd.

Annick Press gratefully acknowledges
the support of The Canada Council and
the Ontario Arts Council.

Canadian Cataloguing in Publication Data

Fernandes, Kim.
    Zebo and the dirty planet

ISBN 1-55037-183-5 (bound). — ISBN 1-55037-180-0 (pbk.)

I. Title.

PS8561.E75Z4 1991   jC813'.54   C91-093697-8
PZ7.F47Ze 1991

The type was set in Futura light by Attic Typesetting Inc.

Distributed in Canada and the USA by:
Firefly Books Ltd.
250 Sparks Avenue
Willowdale, Ontario
M2H 2S4

Printed and bound in Canada
on acid-free paper by D.W. Friesen & Sons

This book is dedicated to all creatures, great and small, who share the fragile planet earth.

ZEBO and the Dirty Planet
by Kim Fernandes

Annick Press, Toronto

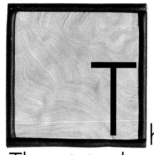his is Zebo's planet.
The air is clean and fresh.
Crystal clear waters gurgle in the streams.
"This is a wonderful planet-home," said Zebo.

Looking through his telescope one day,
Zebo could see that one of the other planets
in the sky was getting quite dirty.
The plants and animals were looking sick.
This made Zebo very sad.
He decided to go and see what was happening.

Zebo climbed into his spaceship
and flew off into the sky.
He went past the stars and over the moon,
until he finally reached the dirty planet.

There was litter on the ground
and garbage in the rivers,
and you could not drink the water.
Now Zebo knew why the animals were looking sick.
"I must do something to help them," he said,
and this is what he did.
Zebo went to very hot places, and very cold places,
places that were very wet, and places
that were very dry.
Onto his spaceship he loaded two
of every kind of animal that was in danger.

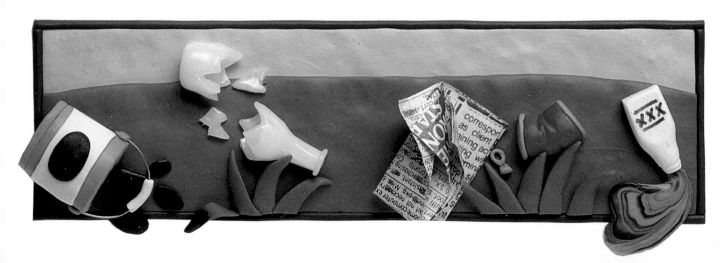

Crocodiles and whooping cranes,
zebras and whales;
tigers and elephants,
and loads and loads of toads.

Zebo flew away from the dirty planet.
Over the moon and past the stars.

Zebo knew that the animals
were snug in their pens.
He did *not* know that Amy and Andrew
had come on board and
were hiding in the closet.
As the spaceship zoomed across the sky,
the children tiptoed out of the closet.

"I wonder where we're going?" said Andrew.
"Are you scared?" asked Amy.
"Of course not!" said Andrew.
"Let's go see the animals."

The children wandered all around the ship
until they came to a door.
"I wonder what's in here?"
said Amy, turning the knob.

Then the spaceship suddenly stopped.
Amy and Andrew ran to the control room.
"We're here!" cried Zebo.
"Where?" asked Amy.
"We're home," said Zebo,
jumping out of his chair.
He ran to the door and opened it wide.
He took a deep breath of the clean, fresh air.
"It's so good to be home again!"

Zebo got busy unloading the animals,
every bird and every beast,

and every creature from the sea.
Quietly, Amy and Andrew helped.

When they were finished,
and the animals were exploring the planet,
Zebo turned to the children and said,
"I don't remember loading you onto the ship.
Who are you?"
"I'm Amy. This is Andrew.
We followed you onto your ship to see
what you were doing with the animals."

"I'm saving them," said Zebo.
"On your planet many kinds
of animals disappear forever."
"Why does this happen?" asked Amy.
"Because," said Zebo,
"Your people are not keeping their planet clean.
They throw garbage in the water.
They chop down too many trees
where the animals live."
This upset Amy and Andrew.
"Can our people fix their planet?" they asked.
"I think so," said Zebo,
"but they have to want to very much."

"Then we must go home," said Andrew.
"We must go home and tell them right away."
"I'll make a list of things we can do," said Amy.
"An excellent idea," said Zebo.
Zebo gave Amy and Andrew a spaceship all their own
and a map of the sky.
"Tell your people," said Zebo,
"That when they learn to take care of the trees
and keep the water clean
then I will bring the animals back."
"We will tell them," said Amy and Andrew
and they set off towards the stars.

The Beginning

Amy and Andrew's list—

If there is a recycling programme in your community, this is what you can do to help:
Save—
glass bottles, (the non-returnable kind);
tin cans, rinsed;
newspapers, after removing shiny inserts with colour printing;
save the funnies, as they make excellent gift wrap;
plastic bottles. Find out which of these can be recycled.

If there is no recycling programme available to you, this is what you can do to start your own:
Save these items, so they can be used again—
rubber bands, string, plastic closing tabs, gift wrap, bows.
Flatten and fold clean paper bags or plastic bags, (then help shoppers in your family remember to take them back to the store).
Other ways in which you can help:
Do not litter;
turn off lights and TV when you leave the room;
bring your own cloth shopping-bag to the store.